Piano Solo
David Lanz
Living Temples
With Gary Stroutsos, Flute

ISBN 978-1-4234-5516-5

HAL•LEONARD® CORPORATION
7777 W. BLUEMOUND RD. P.O. BOX 13819 MILWAUKEE, WI 53213

In Australia Contact:
Hal Leonard Australia Pty. Ltd.
4 Lentara Court
Cheltenham, Victoria, 3192 Australia
Email: ausadmin@halleonard.com.au

For all works contained herein:
Unauthorized copying, arranging, adapting, recording or public performance is an infringement of copyright.
Infringers are liable under the law.

Visit Hal Leonard Online at
www.halleonard.com

SUN CHASERS

By DAVID LANZ

Moderately

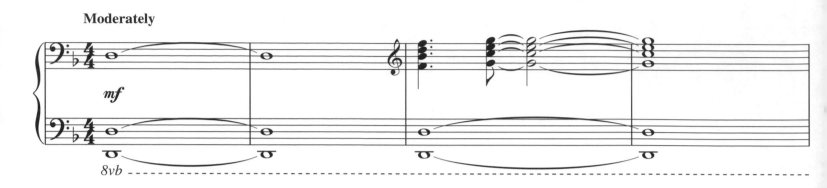

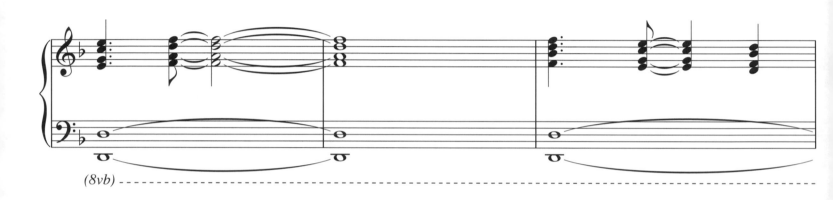

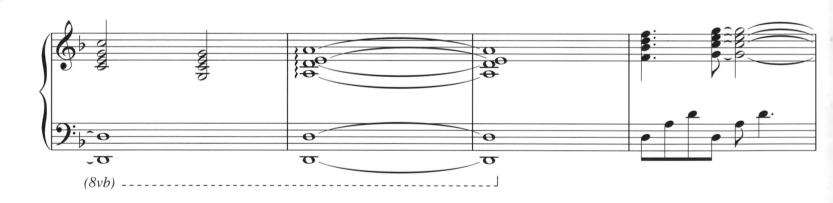

Copyright © 2007 by Moon Boy Music (BMI)
All Rights Reserved   Used by Permission

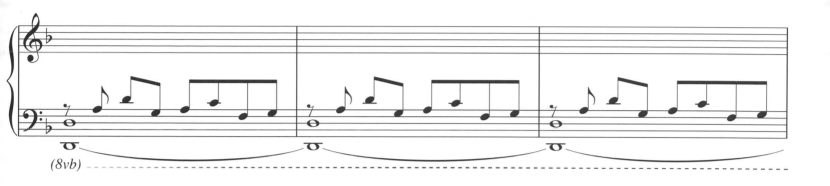

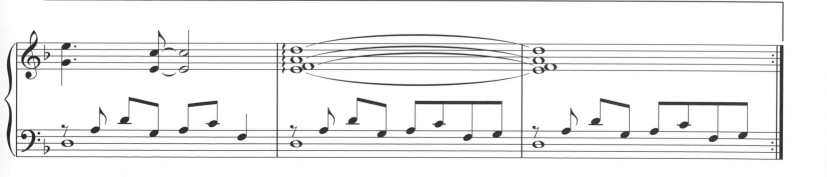

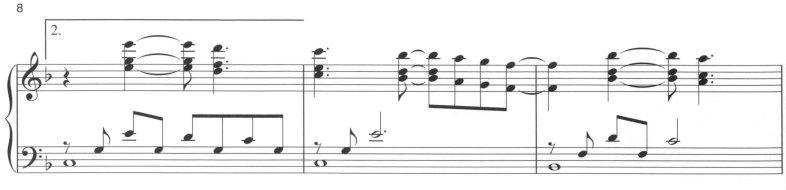

Freely

Tempo I

Very slowly, freely

RIO SAN RAFAEL

By DAVID LANZ

Moderately

With pedal throughout

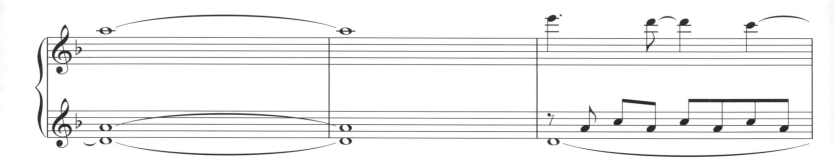

Copyright © 2007 by Moon Boy Music (BMI)
All Rights Reserved   Used by Permission

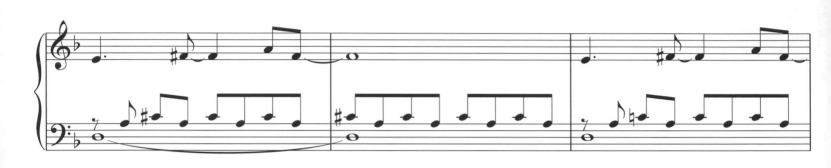

Flute

DESERT STAR

By DAVID LANZ

Slowly, very freely

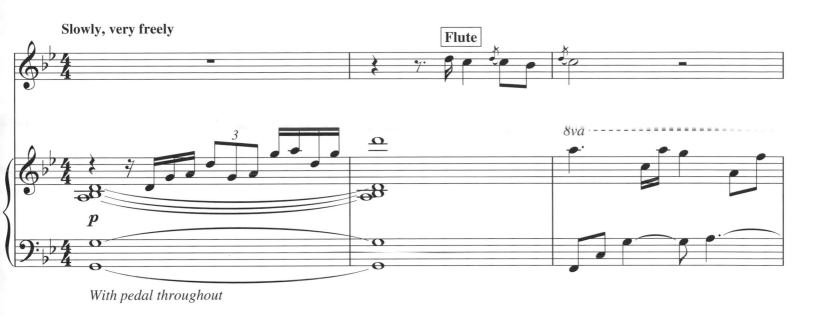

With pedal throughout

Moderately

Flute
(Play 2nd time only)

Copyright © 2007 by Moon Boy Music (BMI)
All Rights Reserved   Used by Permission

Tempo I

RAIN DANCER

By DAVID LANZ

Moderately, with movement

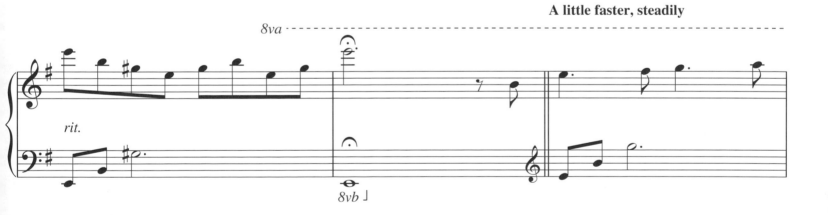

A little faster, steadily

Copyright © 2007 by Moon Boy Music (BMI)
All Rights Reserved   Used by Permission

SEA OF MESCALERO

By DAVID LANZ

Moderately

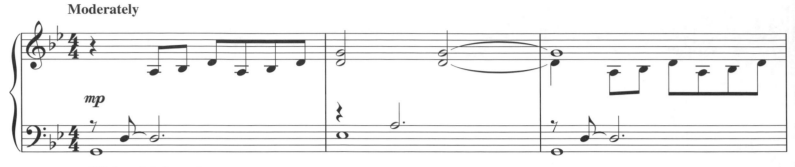

mp

With pedal throughout

Flute

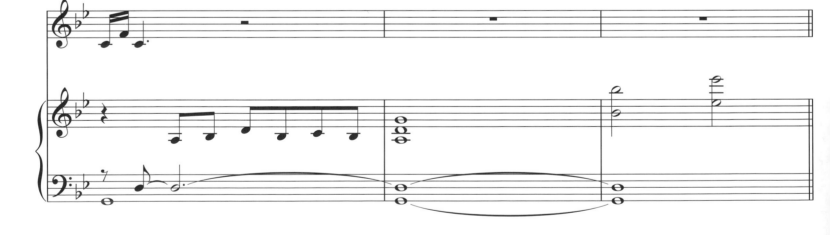

Copyright © 2007 by Moon Boy Music (BMI)
All Rights Reserved   Used by Permission

TEMPLE DANCE

By DAVID LANZ

Copyright © 2007 by Moon Boy Music (BMI)
All Rights Reserved   Used by Permission

Violin

ANCIENT VOICES

By DAVID LANZ
and GARY STROUTSOS

With atmospheric synth accompaniment

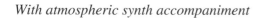

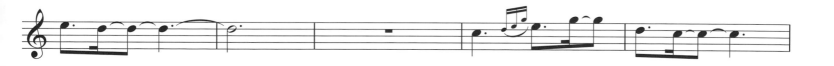

Copyright © 2007 by Moon Boy Music (BMI) and Ko Ko Arts Music (ASCAP)
All Rights Reserved   Used by Permission

WALK IN BEAUTY

By DAVID LANZ
and GARY STROUTSOS

Very slowly, freely

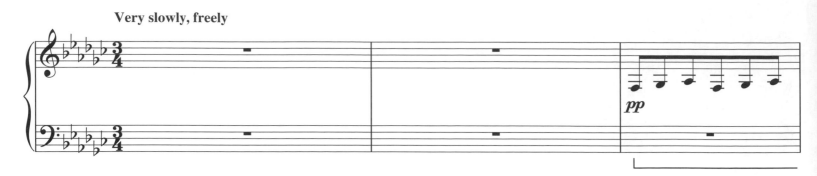

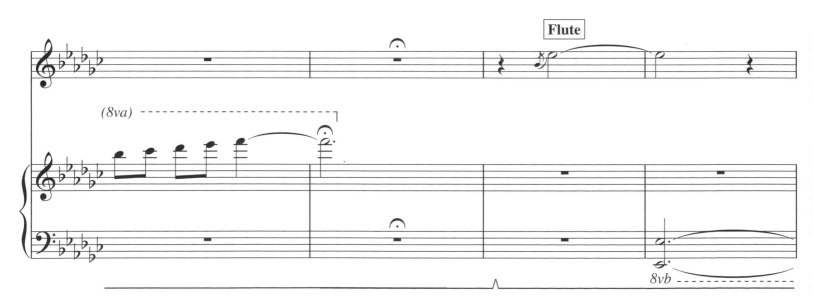

Copyright © 2007 by Moon Boy Music (BMI) and Ko Ko Arts Music (ASCAP)
All Rights Reserved   Used by Permission

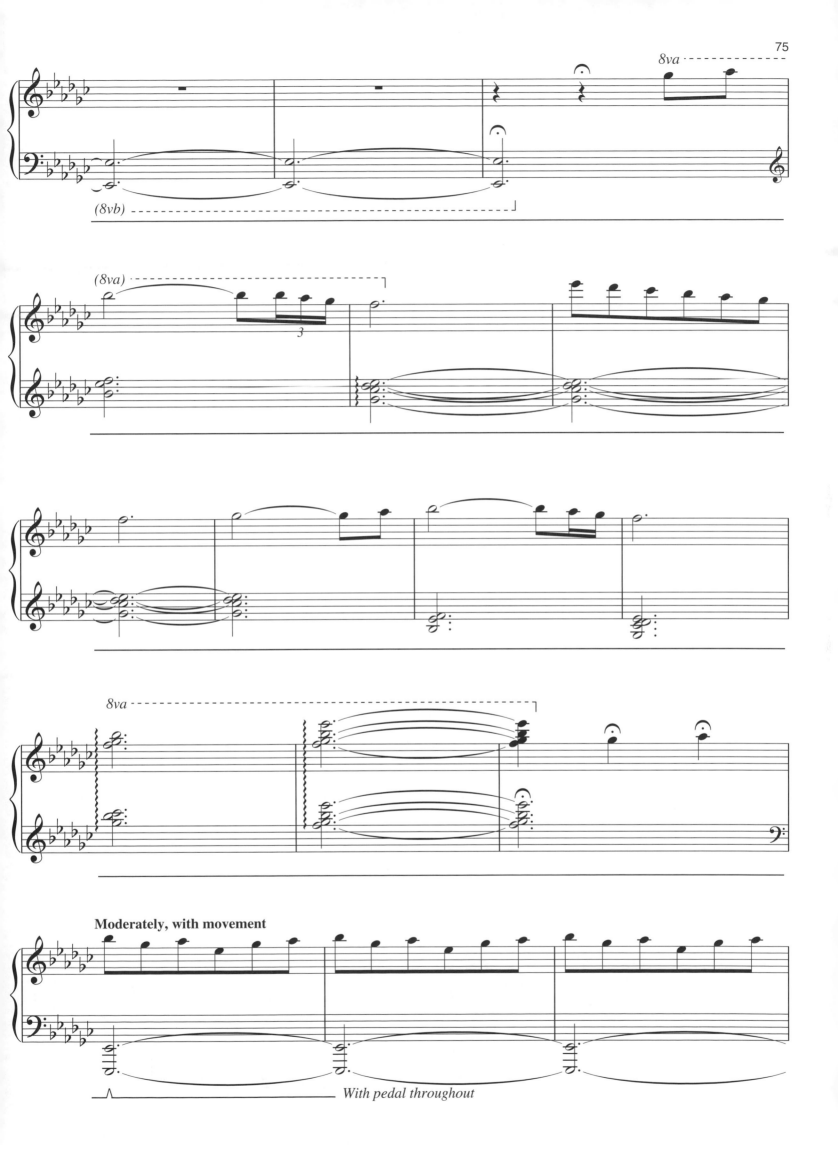

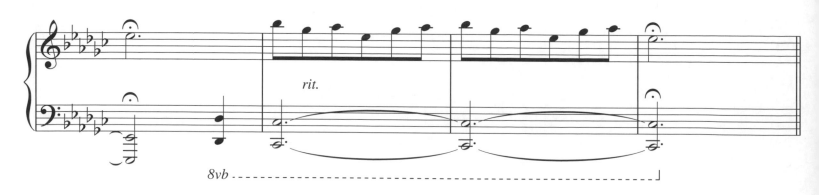

Moderately, steadily

Two Flutes

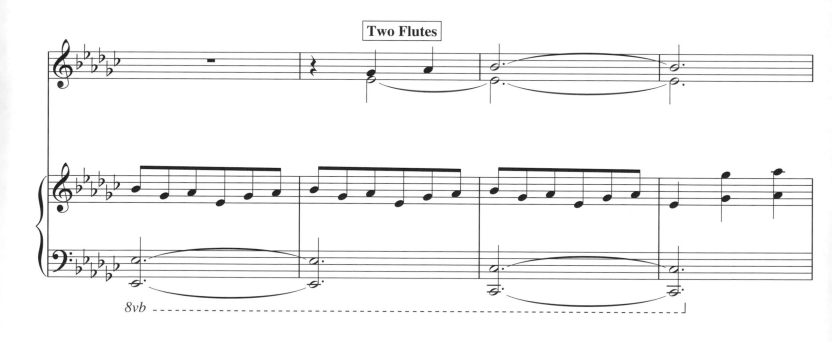

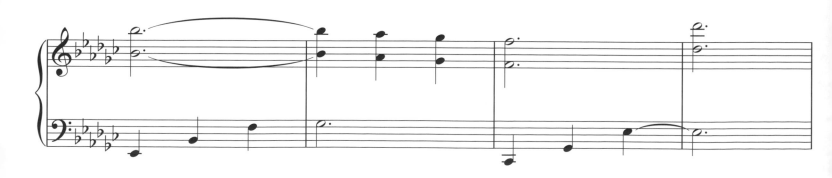

8vb

8vb throughout

Very slowly, freely

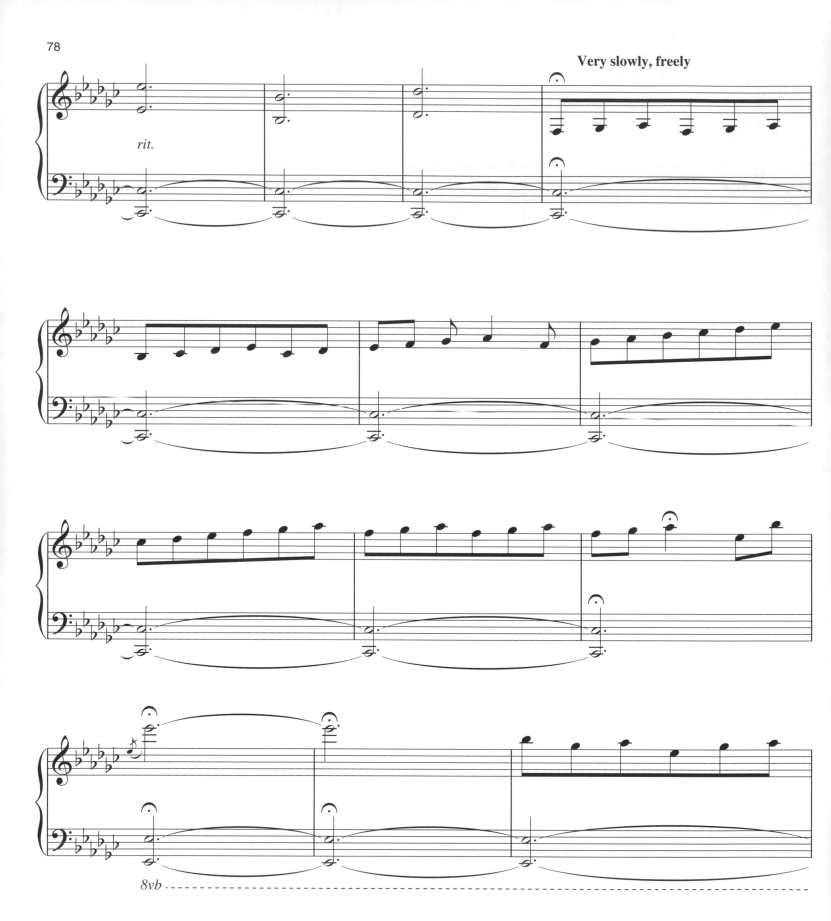

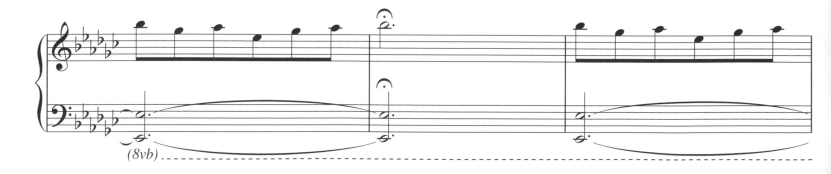

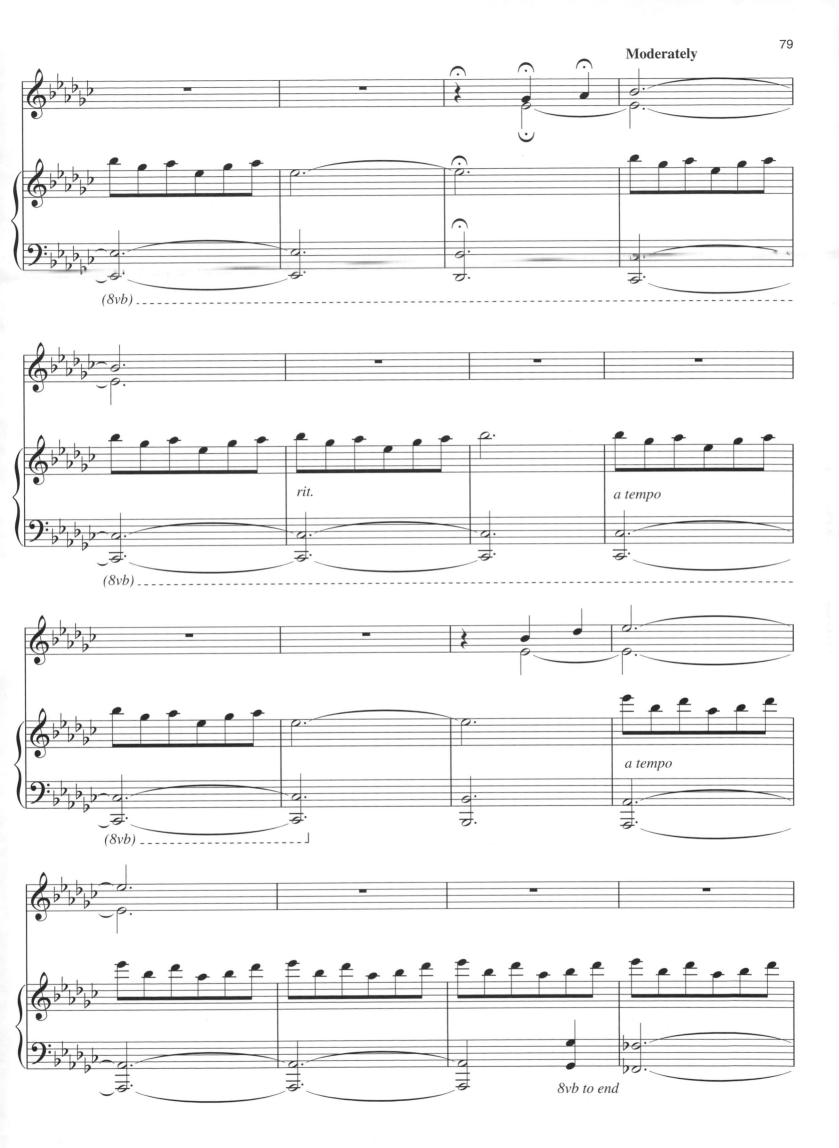

Moderately, steadily

Two Flutes

Repeat and Fade

Optional Ending

LIVING TEMPLES
(Ambient Plains)

By DAVID LANZ

Copyright © 2006 by Moon Boy Music (BMI)
All Rights Reserved   Used by Permission